Songs of Soul

SHRIKRISHNA KULKARNI

BlueRose ONE .com
Stories Matter

First Published in December 2022

ISBN: 978-93-5704-113-3

eISBN: 978-93-5704-575-9

BLUEROSE PUBLISHERS

www.BlueRoseONE.com

info@bluerosepublishers.com

+91 8882 898 898

Cover Design:

Muskan Sachdeva

Typographic Design:

Pooja Sharma

Distributed by: BlueRose, Amazon, Flipkart

Dedication

This collection of poems is dedicated to my wife Rakhi, who has been a source of my inspiration.

Preface

My affinity with poetry started with my understanding of the world and an interest in philosophy. The blend of nature and spirituality is a mystery to feel and depict. From a philosophical standpoint, acquiring wisdom to understand the self from a correct perspective is a question. From a poetic view, we can see that many of the objects in the real world show the impressions of human emotions. The flowers, leaves, butterflies, mountains and rivers invoke different feelings in the mind. This aspect allures me while writing poems. For me, poetry is a manifestation of experience from nature and the inner being. I believe no other form of art can enable feelings to penetrate deeper into the mind than poetry. There is a considerable unexpressed part of human experience, and poetry discovers it and brings it to the conscious part of the mind. That improves our awareness of self and broadens our outlook. Sometimes poems act like a magnifying glass to see the truth hidden in the complex setup of emotions of the mind or understand the reality in each situation.

The poems capture the experiences and perspectives felt at different points in time. The feelings or thoughts at a given time may not agree with the same at the other time. Sometimes it will show contentedness with the world we live in, and sometimes it will show eagerness to fly into the infinite world beyond our limits. Some of the poems raise philosophical enquiries like who am I, what is the purpose of life, where are we destined, what is truth etc. Those poems use analogies or take the recipe from real-world events to show the mysterious nature of inward being. The poems are not restricted to specific philosophies or religious doctrines while expressing the themes because the focus is purely on the inner experience. Nature inspires some of the poems from the small things like wings of butterflies, dew etc. or describes the absorbed state of mind. The poem 'Late in the Night' was composed during the college days to demonstrate the richness of nature experienced by a poor man. There are poems with the theme of love which describe the nature of love, the marvelous feelings and captivated state of mind. I have attempted to bring out the beautiful aspects of life and look at them from poetic perspectives. Many of the poems use a rhyming scheme.

My experience of writing poems has been very satisfying and pleasant. I feel the same when I read others'. I am indebted to the various poets and writers whose books I read and get the inspiration to write. I want to share the same experience with my readers and befriend them. It will fulfil my attempt to publish the work if the poems could knock on the doors of someone's mind. I am opening the store of feelings that I experienced and cherished.

Acknowledgment

My gratitude to Prof. Mohana Nair for guiding me and appreciating. I feel really encouraged by her support.

Contents

For A Moment........13

Day And Night........15

Light… 17

Question Mark........18

Love 19

Soul........20

God Of Innocence........21

Three Stones…! 22

Wings 24

Leaf........25

With The Wildest Imagination........26

Smiling Beauty! 27

Eternity........28

Bird 29

Inner Sky 30

Knowledge........31

Fire Who You Are? 32

Two Dogs........33

Late In The Night........35

Gift 37
Smile 39
Beauty 40
Invite The Fire Of Invisible Spirit 41
Ephemeral 42
Exploration 43
Soul Struggling 44
Oh, Soul! 45
Goddess Of Five Elements 47
Leaf And The Tree 49
Monsoon 51
I Am Sorry! 52
Sphere 54
Life Carrier 55
Self-Image 56
Eagle 57
Fire… 59
Voyage 60
Nest 62
Sky 64
Fear 65
Stuck 66

Lone Traveler 67
Destiny 68
Perpetual 69
Nature's Inspiration 70
Grief 72
Setting Sun Of The Year 74
Nature 75
Dream 76
Turbulent 77
Liars 78
My Own Self 79
Freedom 80
Wanderer 81
Spirit 82
Prayer 83
Hermit 84
Joyous Tree 87
Picture 88
Tree 89
Dew 90
Oh, Love! 91
The Whole And Parts 92

Death, Who Are You? 93
Identity 95
Joy 96
Learned 97
Debris 99
Wisdom 100
Fullmoon 101
Horizon 102
Hope 103
Magnificent Lady! 105
Structure 106
Darkness 107
Drop Of Water 108
Divine Design 109
Ant Heap 110
I Have Faith In 111

For A Moment

I lit up a candle and bowed for a moment,
Light flashed in my heart.
Frailties revealed during struggle with soul,
Friction where I failed, and evil won,
And uncontrolled thoughts,
All vanished.
I know it was for a moment.
I am made incomplete,
My awareness is blended with desires and lust,
So, half of my existence is my own,
And rest half surrenders to subjects,
But now I am complete and whole; I felt.
I know it was for a moment.
I felt I touched eternity,
I am in the realm of the soul,
I have infinite prowess over the mind,
I have attained inner peace,
Pure love was my sole passion.
I know it was for a moment.
With that one moment of prayer,
I could focus my wandering mind,
I could extend where I failed to reach,

I realized wholeness and restrained senses,

Felt, purity, purpose and passion.

The magic of the moment's action,

I know it was forever…!

Day And Night

Day said, 'In my light, do
The ocean waves roar and glisten
And when I dawn, birds twitter and
I wake up the people and enlighten them,
Such is my glory.'

Night said, 'The light is
In a dormant store in my womb
And upon its eruption, you are born,
But I do exist alongside eternity,
Both of us have no birth.'

Day said, 'In my light, do the poets
See the world and sing, and
The sages conceive the notions and forms
Revealing the truth,
You blind them and make them wander.'

Night said, 'You are clad with light
Otherwise, you are also in eternal darkness.
You are felt because I do
Contrast you.'

Spoke eternity, in the twilight and dawn,
'When both of you fade,
The wise shall meditate on me.
The mystery is but an interplay of
Day and night,
I have a spell from the very bottom
Where the truth resides.'

Light...

The light was travelling through the dark,
From where it had left, there was no mark.
At the time of birth was a mystical spark...
New life in cells to embark.

Flashes of light appeared in my mind.
What is perpetual in the body to find?
Store of self, mind and intellect of kind
For my living, what works from behind?

Who am I, and where am I destined to go?
What began at birth that will end so?
There were moments of flashes though
Bathed in the light for answers to know.

In what form shall I be after I die?
Will I be aware and with free will fly?
Be the light to travel in the dark sky?
Will there still be who, what and why?

Question Mark

Long street stretching sight,
Diminishing distant end of it,
Post lamps on either side compete,
Feet move on the road concrete.

Rains making shining ground,
Nothing else but a wet sound,
End in illusion, turning round,
Where only a question mark is found.

Breeze moist hint at the creation,
Ending trails of past depression,
The Road straight ahead does mention,
New answers to the same old question.

What is in the end? I don't know.
Why am I walking? Neither do I know.
Tomorrow sky shall come with a rainbow.
Questions are friends, and ideas flow.

Love

I don't need to drink and turn my eyes blind.
To the stories of the past that constantly rewind,
Thy mere presence appeals the love,
And I get a gush of wine from the very depths of my mind.

Every time I see you, I meet a fresh novice,
I look at you and then down, have glances twice.
When eyes meet, I see a flash of lightning and an aura of a kind,
Mind melting, overwhelming feelings and noiseless voice.

I experience a goddess half human and half fish,
Floating in front of the eye of the mind and asking for a unique wish.
To be true to myself, I am no longer,
In a state to express and ask, looking into those eyes, bluish.

I don't need anything, I say, and I feel content.
I can't get rid of this state of constant reinforcement,
Of love, sick heart and images of the event,
I do live in the fort of love, in an uncommon tent.

Soul

Skeleton of bones, covered with flesh.
Net of veins, carrying blood fresh.

Web of nerves, many secretors within.
The whole of the body is wrapped in the skin.

Beats of the heart, lungs constant respiring.
The flow of the lifeblood is never ever interrupting.

Outside environment, feelings, and sensations,
State of mind and external temptations.

Unseen hidden in me, dwelling in this whole,
I am not a part of it, but playing a central role.

Keep account of the actions, wrong and right,
My own mind with myself has a constant fight.

Have many acquaintances and do relate to others,
Still, I am alone amidst many friends and peers.

I am in my brain and mind, inside this whole body.
Still, I am nowhere existing but caught in this custody!

God Of Innocence

Oh, God of innocence,
You spread on the face of a newborn,
Magic that brings affection!
Its cry and laughter,
You fill with an appeal to the mother.
You tell the fairy tale in the dreams,
Full of animals, birds, and fairy themes.
You dwell in everything tiny.
Wherever you reflect, get admirers many.
You are in the calf, kid, puppy and chick,
And those all getting into mother's lap quick.
You are in a tiny plant just sprouting,
And like a tall tree acting!
You may remain in the mind of elders,
Who, with age, just got bolder!
Bless me so that I preserve a child in me,
Face the challenges by invoking thee.
Bless me, the innocence that I embrace, in essence,
Let it reflect in every sense!

Three Stones...!

Three stones were laid.
One represented the lower body,
Second the upper, the face and head,
Third the middle trunk.
Water was sprinkled,
Something came into being,
Uncontrolled waves spinning around the head,
Then forming around the middle,
Then the portion lower,
Then woke up the invisible body,
Invisible became the stones there!

Said, I am the ghost eternal,
I find the places abnormal,
The disturbance is my passion,
Inflicting pains my mission,
Purposeless mind my residence,
Disturbed sight my evidence,
I shut down your mind,
Close the windows,
I accept a contradiction,
My stories are fiction,

I spin circles of thoughts,
There is no conclusion,
Hallucination and illusion,
Justice led by ego,
Disharmony of inner space,
In conflicts, I leave a trace,
Don't sprinkle greedy water on me,
You shall reduce to three stones, you see!

Wings

Wings of the butterfly move in the air,
A faint feeling came into my aching mind somewhere,
I entered in trance and existed merely,
Wonder what is carrying it there and here.

Touch them for a moment and feel touchless,
Run behind them, too and feel bodiless.
It sat on a flower and arrested me effortlessly,
O, that flying mystic life made me speechless!

Rested on a flower and suck some sweet,
Competing for the painting on wings of it,
Little flower kiss it one momentary treat,
I stood lost totally on the empty street.

How does it know where it has to go?
What to do? Does it really know?
Can my mind wear the wings gently so?
And fly in moments harsher, though?

Leaf

Leaf of a tree falling on the ground,
Parted from the tranquil tree with no sound,
Speechless with grief, the tree with leaves around,
Sorrowful, sad, poignant moment and silent background.

Like a mother, tree winced at the moment of departure,
When the beloved parted whom, it did nurture,
Left a tear at the joint, a painful rupture,
Leaving a wound, a tiny feature forever and ever.

The leaf fell on the ground and rested there,
Green for a day, and then yellow acquire.
Last wet moments and then on the fire,
Leaving the implicit, unspoken desire.

Was it a life hanging on the tree?
Or linked with roots but existed free?
Lasting for a season and then agree,
To the wild nature's final decree.

With The Wildest Imagination

With the wildest imagination,
Would have failed to draw,
The glimpse of thee that I saw,
It is not of colours, lines or hue,
But the spirit and appealing view.

My fingers would fail to catch,
Smiley moist spread on thy face,
Where the goddess of beauty left her trace,
Mixed with rays borrowed from the moon,
On the saturated skin for admirers, a boon.

On the figure that flies in space,
My worldly sight would fail to rest,
On a dancing figure with a divine crest,
The glow was alluring, crushing me inside,
It is beyond me the state to avoid.

Smiling Beauty!

Oh, smiling beauty,
Blooming in the class!
Thou stole my heart!
Oh, Sweet Venus,
Let me smell thy blossom!
Let me have at least,
A glance of thy lucid eyes!
Let me have at least,
A touch of the figure that flies!
Oh, cuckoo of spring,
Let me hear the whistle,
That utter thy lips!
Oh! Goddess bless me,
In the whirligigs of time,
I should never lose thee!
Oh, darl, be a thunderbolt,
And fall on me,
Let me be,
One with thee!

Eternity

The cells of my body are dwelling,
In the unseen, eternal thing.
Beyond the matter of the body, making
Presence, which awareness confirms.

That observes feelings come and go,
And sees the burning desire grow.
It pulls me into that eternal flow,
Can the mind dissolve in that mystical glow?

What is the origin of a flower's smile?
Where is it hidden in its style?
Is it eternal in the trees and the soil?
Or is it a brief flash lasting for a while?

Is it my mere faith that I exist?
Is awareness giving it a wiser twist?
Do the spirit and matter coexist?
Is it bestowed by the supreme artist?

Bird

There is an immortal bird in me,
It starves for the moonlight,
Pure milky and pollute-free,
It drinks in the night silvery.
Originating from the spirit bright,
Emitting the moonlight.
When it is intoxicated,
It transcends passions, thoughts and instincts,
It just observes good, bad, bitter and sweet,
Happiness, Joys, sorrows and feelings are distinct,
And it keeps on drinking and further intoxicates
Then it loses sense of everything,
The character, tastes, moods and all that,
Its eyes see only light,
And the mind is filled with only light,
It loses the distinction between light and the moon.
It becomes the moon,
All converge into one!

Inner Sky

That which decays dissolves upon death,
My mind, body, and wealth,
Things that vary with time disappear,
What will be the remain am not sure.

What is at the beginning that changes after death?
I follow destiny and the path with faith,
What is perpetual during the course?
Does actuality alter after living, suffering and remorse?

My guts don't accept I will be no more after I die.
I am everything in my infinite, inner sky.
Am not mixed with the matter, force and light,
My sky has no colours and is neither dark nor bright.

My coming to being might have one cause or multiple,
But I shall be without a notion or a form and single,
I shall dwell in myself, covered by myself and intangible,
I shall float and fly and grow and shrink, though infinitesimal.

Knowledge

Potter created the pot out of clay,
And He filled knowledge in it.
He gave words to express,
To mean, share and not display.

For in whatever quantity you show,
It is zero compared to infinite,
That would insult the very filler,
And belittle the one displaying it.

He gave the knowledge to discover,
But he blocked all the ways,
Hidden identity and disappear.
He went beyond nights and days.

One day the pot might crack,
Wisdom shall be sucked back,
Knowledge shall meet its apt form.
You are but you, after the life storm!

Fire Who You Are?

Oh, Fire!
You make buds out of stars.
Wreathed the universe with the milky way,
And billions of such galaxies.
What are you, indeed? I call it a fire.
Often, I see you,
In the spark or a flame,
Smouldering under the surface,
Emitting an ember,
In connection with the matter.
This is what I see and feel you.
In spirit, what are you?
Are you cool or hot or beyond that?
You boil the water,
Or keep it frozen in ice.
You are dormant everywhere.
And also, in the forest fire.
Do you really go out?
Or are you ever-present?
I want to see you and hold,
In your exact form,
That you were before the universe,
When the five elements were in their original form,
Before they mixed and fashioned the universe.

Two Dogs

There was a stray dog.
It had sore skin, dirt and scars,
As if orphan pains.
And there was a dog walking
Tied to a belt in the hand of a woman,
With cleanly washed and dried furs.
She moved her softer fingers,
Through his silky hair,
Giving a parental touch and warmth.
Soon their eyes meet each other,
Belligerence was in both similar,
Started barking at disputes about territory.
Over time somehow, became friends with each other.
The tame dog said,
'Food tastes better when acquired with effort,
When available with ease becomes routine,
And lose the charm and thrill of hunger.'
The stray dog said,
'See the pains I have to bear for food,
Sometimes a wicked person throws a stone at me,
Sometimes a kind man offers me food,
I have to feast on the waste and bones of the dead too.'

The tame dog said,
'We have to think before barking and biting,
We need to civilize like men,
A day will come when all men will adopt us,
And love us like members of their family.'
The stray dog said,
'What about our territories,
And what about our self-respect,
Look at the belt that is tied around your neck,
Sophistication, I agree, but our domain,
Why learn it from men and enchain?
Our soul shines in freedom. Why civilize in vain?'
The tame dog said,
'To enjoy liberty and reign in the hell,
Or enjoy the luxuries and enslave in heaven,
A wise will choose the latter, no question!'
The stray dog said,
'You befriend the men and me, the nature,
And there is a heaven in my inner sphere.
Wise or not, I don't know, my dear!'

Late In The Night...

The milky moon mounted in the sky,
Twinkling stars all way around,
Poorest man with the richest soul,
Was lying on the ground.

Blowing breeze passing through leaves,
Fast asleep, everything in sight,
No room for him to worry,
Still sleepless late in the night.

Tired streets taking rest,
Beneath the post lamp, warming them,
A short blanket covered him half,
Still feeling warmth, from where it came?

Silent buildings, silent was everything.
Mixed with darkness was the milk of the moon.
Relaxed, his body and mind,
Being amidst silent stars and moon.

His eyes were filled with the scene.
Ears were listening to the leaves.
A man dumb in despair was enjoying the rich.
How can one easily believe?

Aware of everything but himself,
Rich was he, richer than anybody,
Late night absorbed us into sleep,
Richer we poorer than him, a tragedy!

Gift

The smell of the soil at the beginning of the monsoon,
Arising creativity, the season's gift and nature's boon.

Encapsulated tranquil light pouring from the moon,
Soothing the mind and inspiring nature's songs soon.

The clear sky in autumn and tiny stars blinking.
Bright rays of the heavenly bodies, mortals are drinking.

The chirping of the birds coming out of crowded plants,
The fresh mind of the musical morning celebrates in chants.

Emptying the mind and refilling, the flower's scent doing magic,
Ending the stress and strain, making the mind so energetic.

Small children clapping hands upon seeing the drops of rain,
The gush of energy comes into the mind, overcoming the pain.

A flock of birds are flying in curves near the horizon in the distant sky,
A wave of feeling in the mind that raises wings and attempts to fly.

The rising and setting sun with the sky acquiring multiple colours,

Transiting times helps discover the depths of the mind and its layers.

Smile

Smile with slanted eyes,
With lips making a slight curve,
Thrilled every cell of my body,
Pleasant signals through every nerve.

The trunks of green trees,
Nodded with a push of wind,
What magic the universe plays and,
A smile echoed in nature's mind.

Who sent you at this time and place?
What made my eyes meet yours?
That is more than mere coincidence,
Made to meet the whole of inner spheres.

Why did we meet and have to depart,
Am I to forget and move on again?
Can I freeze at that moment in ecstasy?
Why does destiny create events in vain?

Beauty

Something is continuously streaming from within,
Channelized through tunnels of purity,
Reflected in the eyes and on the face, a layer thin,
Of innocence that scatters nothing but beauty.

Surprised where the beauty comes from,
Some without appeal but childish charm.
Marked the faces whom many admired,
Innocence from the depth of mind to the face wired.

A glimpse that arises affection,
The gesture that arrests attention,
Compelling to follow the delicate feather,
So effortlessly flying in the air.

Actions, speech and smile of mine,
Be filled with that innocence, divine.
Dreams of a soul struggling to survive,
May it be free to sustain and strive?

Invite The Fire Of Invisible Spirit

Invite the fire of the invisible spirit,
Hold it in the middle of your heart,
Feel thy existence engulfed in it,
Ego and self, melt in the heat.

Values, virtue and nature are innate,
Instincts, passions and many traits,
The memories are bitter and sweet,
Beliefs, faith and all that with truth intersect.

Beauties are alluring and survival threats,
To acquire and gain constant fight,
Presentiments sudden of fearful fate,
Altar of wisdom and truth secret.

Truth is where every line meets,
Flows of ideals with furore greet,
All the deeds with flaws retreat,
In the heart where holy fire lit.

Ephemeral

Life is like a continuous line,
With mysteries joining dots,
Or events that destiny defines,
At the junction, subtle thoughts.

Coming to life for a moment,
With every breath that I borne,
The root of existence to invent,
Pumped in the cells worn.

A lot is there in a moment,
A connection with the future and past.
I do live in the present,
And hope, anxiety, and trails of loss.

Process of continued living,
Despite after loss and gain.
Mystery of observer driving,
Embrace moments and entertain.

Exploration

Listen to the silence,
There is an echo from within.
Words aspire to make a presence,
Struggle to say what they mean.

Look deeper into the invisible,
Image of self-coming in sight,
In the inner space, unreachable,
Like galaxies pouring bright.

Can't touch thc intangible,
Neither can smell the odourless,
Within my limit, I am capable,
Though to find myself body less.

No dimensions measure me.
Neither coordinate locate me.
Still, I exist, I do feel,
In the centre of an unknown wheel.

Soul Struggling

My heart does not beat at my will,
In the body no flesh I do fill,
I think it is my body, mind and free will,
I dwell, exist, and sort of that still.

Never expressed to be born at my wish,
Still, I think it's my life and my own anguish,
And can't just fly and say all this can finish,
In the colourless sky but to the eyes bluish.

Pride of being a person and the ego within,
The Ill-defined notion of existence therein.
Is it all my ignorance that reign?
That I think and do and whatever I mean.

What is it that am I searching for?
In the end, everything I am dumping,
Truth, a question mark inscribed and pains tingling,
Only eternal gift of God and the soul struggling.

Oh, Soul!

You are the ultimate realization in mind,
What I learn is just an invocation of your preexisting prowess,
What I express is just your unsung song,
What I articulate is just your inspiration,
What I reveal is just your mystery.
I offer the oblation of thoughts on the altar of wisdom,
My mind, intellect is an instrument at your disposal.
Words fail to compose verses for you,
You are the inspiration to define words for things.
You are neither thing nor a concept,
I can't denote you as single or multiple,
You are in the force of willpower.
You give me a powerful surge in my willpower,
You are the spark in the friction of thoughts,
Which controls the mind and leads it.
You dwell inside parts and also encompass the whole.
When you arise, weak thoughts are driven out.
When there are clouds of doubt,
Except for darkness, nothing in sight,
The self is not able to find any route,
I perform the prayer and invoke you.
You are energy in all my struggles and fight.

When the darkness fills the mind, you are a firefly,

When I am calm, you are the joy.

Allow the light to penetrate from you, O, soul!

Let my passions withstand the wind!

Let the pursuit of perfection be the sole purpose!

Goddess Of Five Elements

The Goddess of the five elements is pouring,
In the gaped mouth of ether,
The fire and other elements,
In an attempt to satiate,
Unquenchable thirst of
Ether to expand and grow infinite.

The Goddess of the five elements is pouring,
In the gaped mouth of fire,
The matter and other elements,
In an attempt to satiate,
Unquenchable thirst of,
Fire to conquer and grow wild.

The Goddess of the five elements is pouring,
In the gaped mouth of matter,
The water and other elements,
In an attempt to satiate,
Unquenchable thirst of,
Matter to seed and grow life.

The Goddess of five elements is pouring,
In the gaped mouth of water,
The air and other elements,
In an attempt to satiate,
Unquenchable thirst of,
Water to flow (in the skies) and flourish life.

The Goddess of five elements is pouring,
In the gaped mouth of life,
Fire, ether, water, air, matter,
In an attempt to satiate,
Unquenchable thirst of,
Life to sense and grow inward!

Leaf And The Tree

A tender green leaf sprouting,
So innocently was moving with stem,
The smallest was it and fascinating,
Became shivery when airflow came.

With its grip on the branch increasing,
It was confident, moving with ease,
Turned mature green and befriended breeze,
Day by day was growing in size.

In summer, it was green with a rich style,
Got wet in the monsoon with a cheerful smile,
In heavy rains, it survived and acted agile,
Come winter, life around became volatile.

It shivered with cold and saw its colours changing,
Became pale and saw more signs of ageing,
The present was dull but could keep engaging,
With memories of past seasons and imaging.

A sudden breeze detached it from the tree,
With body tossing, it fell on the earth,
From the bodily life, it became free,
Merged in the soil for the rebirth.

Slowly the tree shed all its leaves,
The winter snowfall covered it,
It was a bare tree, as anyone believes,
But it started penance in the true spirit.

Monsoon

Creepers clinging to the stone,
Descending from top to the ground,
Where again, the shrub is grown,
Monsoon-blessed greenery abounds.

Plateau turned parrot green,
Proud stones gossip secrets keen,
With trees scarcely spread,
With flowers yellow, white and red.

Dark clouds and heavy rains,
Trickles flow, water drains,
Green is getting clear and clean,
The soul is smiling, in the freshness seen.

Seasons carry secrets of the soul,
Changes colours of the nature whole,
Cycles reveal the progress and goal,
In search of the purpose sole.

I Am Sorry!

I know your longing for me was extreme.
Your lips were shivering,
Gaze had been hesitating,
And penetrated,
To the bottom of my mind.

I had to leave you,
I had my own engagements,
And you had your necessities,
You were right, I appreciate.
I know that you were lonely,
Devoid of love forever,
But I could not promise you,
Could not fill your passion and loneliness.

My mind was quaking,
On departing you,
Winds were flowing against,
I was walking half-heartedly,
For my body was walking ahead,
And my mind was dragging behind.
I know my soul had won,

But I lost,
Whether one value wins or the other,
I was indeed losing on all counts,
I am sorry!

Sphere

Reddish disc in the morning east,
Mixing warmth in the air and mist,
Ascending in the sky, giving a yellow twist.
Days and nights awake my consciousness, a priest.

When I feel past, present and future,
Exclusive dimensions and the thoughts pure,
Something more than the instincts, mere,
In my heart appear an ever-growing mind-sphere.

Arrows are shot of actions and words,
Streams of thoughts and the crossing swords,
Dance of the evil and musical chords,
Self and reason serving satanic lords.

Shadows of fear and faint images,
In the end, everything averages,
Faded spirit and sickness of ages,
Above all, the wisdom of sages.

Right and wrong conflicting flows,
Mixing streams and pattern glows,
Truth from inside sending beams,
Mysterious sphere of life, where it goes?

Life Carrier

As life moves on,
You get more and more things to miss,
It is the future that we always kiss,
Past remain memories, full of bliss.

Life moves as a carrier wave,
Riding events flowing with time,
All that we wish and crave,
Feel, act, and think sublime.

Same wave as a bright beam,
Or a comet leaving the trail,
And heading toward a future theme,
Can death make it derail?

Birth, growth, decline, and disappear,
The only constant is this carrier,
Existence-sphere of light force and fire,
To later contract into an unknown container.

Self-Image

Delusion of the whole existence, whirling around,
An unknown hidden self at the centre I found,
Something awakening from inside profound,
The invisible is talking without any sound.

It talks, listens, laughs, and has deep feelings,
Sometimes reigns and wears the hat of controlling,
It mixes with others and makes its presence appealing,
Can vanish itself, disappear and has beliefs compelling.

I exist, and so is my image in the mirror,
I have free will, and I am a doer,
The image and the real how do they differ?
Is there any difference for the outside viewer?

The world is dreamy, and the self alone is real,
I am carrying my body to see the world as ideal,
Realize in mind the existence of spiritual,
I wish I dwell in the sphere that is ethereal.

Eagle

Eagle in my mind watches,
All that is decaying and changing,
From the Store of memory fetches,
Memories from the beginning.

It flies above the ground vast,
And looks at broader space,
Whatever the events of the past,
Feels pleasant with time's grace.

The eagle does not feel,
The past sorrows or discomfort,
Or rewinds any past reel,
Of what I lost and what I got.

The eagle is my free self,
Inspects the moments neutrally.
It just keeps on the shelf,
Events that occur naturally.

Moments pass by, that watches the eagle,
With a still and empty mind,
Feelings come and go feeble,
Denies involvement of any kind.

It's a hermit sitting idle,
Exists on its own,
Fed from the spring divine,
A source is scarcely known.

Fire...

A Holy fire within and around,
Space-time matter making ground.

Cells of the body and my soul,
Blazing spirit in parts and whole.

Roots of thought deep in the water,
Passions feelings dream for the better.

Channels of belief and silent streams,
Awareness sends deeper beams.

Dwell in fire, tired self, torn within,
Body, noisy weary parts therein.

Can I stop it and throw it for a while,
Retire to fire and discover the smile?

Rid it of fear, friction and grief,
With the touch of that fire brief.

Voyage

Something was terminating while enroute,
Some fire inside was being blown out,
Was null and void, within, and worn out,
He left the village and kept walking throughout.

The storm was moving towards the village,
Carrying on its head the time-old garbage,
Without turning, he continued the voyage,
He was accustomed to the storm with age.

Half of the reality was that of the day,
Another half was what dark night display,
As if the glow-worm enlightens and conveys,
The deep and strange fables that are at play.

He rested against a trunk, with legs swollen,
Eyes turned red but fearless, and face not sullen,
Feeling dizzy, village revolving around, ignorance-ridden,
The garbage of beliefs and struggles befallen.

The village, storm, glow-worm, day, and night,
In the darkness came the pleasant moonlight,
Cutting the darkness, a beam came out of him, bright,
Leaving the body, he got up with a beam of silver white.

Now he does not have the labour and doesn't have to sweat,
Without five elements, no appetite and no weight,
On his voyage, he started in the galaxies straight,
Even into the skies far beyond this universe, great.

Nest

A frame was mounted on the wall slight obliquely,
Of a painting depicting a flock of birds so uniquely,
A space between the frame and the corner quickly,
Used by birds for a nest that fits them perfectly.

The bird was flying back and forth to get the grass,
Overcoming difficulties that it came across,
The tiny building blocks for the nest to amass,
The straw in its beak got one in every pass.

With restless efforts to complete the endeavour,
The bird was finally inside the natural incubator,
Motherly warmth and hatching were there,
The hardship and the joy motivated by nature.

Innocent chirps filled the fresh morning,
The mother was busy collecting food for the offspring,
Everywhere the joy of creation prevailed,
Nature's play is what birds were singing.

Alas! The sweeper saw and threw it in the waste,
And there were many eggs broken and died the rest,
"To save the frame, you have broken the living nest!"
You love the picture and abandon the genuine guest.

Sky

During the day, the sky clad with many colours,
Keep on altering with the passage of hours,
Gently awakening the birds and the flowers,
To welcome the dawn, tender blue it acquires.

With red disk climbing on the horizon,
A grand smile spreads with the rising sun.
To greet morning to the earth down,
And watches the never-ending life mission.

The day continues its journey slow,
Pieces of cloud red, brown and yellow,
The reflection in the dews down below,
As if they watch and say hello.

When it is rainy, gather clouds dark,
A rainbow with seven colours makes a mark,
Embodied in the sky for creation to spark,
Earth is motivated for life to embark.

Fear

Stars spread infinitely over the night sky,
Ocean was roaring still with waves high,
Horizon is not in sight, and the sleepy earth shy,
On the beach was still lingering a poor boy.

His eyes reflected the dark scene and the fear.
The mind is filled with mystery and loneliness,
There was no one else but a stray dog near.
His eyes show the appetite, the ages-old hunger.

Bent slightly at the top was a coconut tree,
Welcoming the water at the beach with glee,
Slightly contrasting the scene with feelings of eerie,
Ghostly darkness had a whispery dialogue with the sea.

The sand touch, too, gave a strange feeling,
Sense of danger sent to the brain, pains tingling,
The perpetual fear in his mind was signaling,
He then ran away from the sea, roaring.

Stuck

I stopped, turned and saw behind,
Two eyes were awaiting,
Eagerness and depth of mind,
Were reflected in the eyes, gratifying.

That moment deeply stuck,
In mind for many days ahead.
All the feelings were suck,
By the lone memory, the mind did tread.

There was a strong desire,
To experience the occurrence again,
Feel every aspect of the beauty,
And the charm that I saw then.

There was lengthy time passed by,
Suffered a lot of pain but did not meet her again,
I wonder it did happen in the first place, why?
And blame me being so insane.

Lone Traveler

The road is too long, and the destination is not sure,
The dense fogs of suspicion make matters unclear,
Walking becomes easy when I become, in fact, unaware,
Though moving was obvious, the meaning was not easier.

Complex impulses come like a rush of a whirlwind,
Many secrets are hidden deep inside the mind,
Drove me to the acts, don't know what is behind,
Bends and twists come across that I do unwind.

I have been waiting for a long, someone with whom I can share,
Lonely traveller, I am and my destiny, who else shall care?
Being alone caused annoyance, but that is the way here,
Came alone, walked alone and am going alone to where?

Nature is dancing, with all its elements, five,
Beatings of my heart and my living so naive,
Entrapped in all the matters and making sure to thrive,
No destination or origin, am I just nature's captive.

Destiny

Oh Destiny, what is in store for me? You speak not why?
Accumulated Fatigue of the years passing by,
Nothingness and the null in mind with feelings dry,
Life is taking dreadful stances and strange images that fly.

I am awakening you to relieve me am so desperate,
Every thought in the weakened mind poses a new threat.
Rays of hope arise and diminish, and a dark void is met.
Why were you so impassive when you designed my fate?

Swings of the mood and restless mind,
Ghosts of the past stories are constantly behind,
Is it the whole story that my mind does unwind,
It is written by you with upheavals of such a kind.

A puzzled mind is stuck like a deep ocean but still,
Words shall reach the limit and lose their thrill,
My actions and life, nothing but follow your will,
You compose the script, dictate, and I perform the drill.

Perpetual

Oh, Goddess of pleasures perpetual!
Bestow me the love eternal,
Senses to feel others need emotional,
Acumen to strive for purity and rational.

Oh, Lady of Virtues! Arise me from the sleep,
Help me get out of the lust rooted deep,
Free me from guilt, and in solitude, weep.
Let me be generous and prepare promises to keep.

Oh, spirit behind thoughts and actions right!
Let apt be chosen and come in sight,
In the perfection of work, let me find delight,
Bestow me a fraction of thy spirit and might.

Oh, Goddess! Let me pray to you and remember,
In every moment when I can't see clear,
When the ground is slippery, thy virtues I bear,
And for purifying the mind, I shed one tear!

Nature's Inspiration

A river with a deep murmur meandering,
Souls of the birds singing songs at will,
Clouds revealing moods of the sky,
Wandering high above with a liberal feel.
A mountain silent in its place,
No one stole its abode for ages,
It is free of worries and stresses,
With a cover of green opulence.
A man wandering in despair,
Lost in the worldly affairs,
Overlooked mountain and river,
The secret of their free behaviour.
Climbed the mountain,
And thought to jump from the height,
To end his life's tribulation,
But how to end quickly was still a question.
He went to the river,
To jump and reach its depth,
And to come back not forever.
Waited for a moment, despite the fact he dared.
What shall lie to the depth of the vale and bottom of the river?
A corpse. Devastated bodily and morally forever.

Where shall the disdained soul go?
Look at the clouds in the sky,
As if to your soul, they wave 'Hi'.
The spirit of skies is asking to free,
Sense of possession and worry,
Like the flowing river,
Like the mountain standing ever
Plantation and green trees,
As natural and as free.
Where shall your struggle go so far?
To change your tiny world, you are,
To shape its dreams and future.
He was able to see the message clear
From the mountain, clouds and river.
He returned to face life with vigour,
Without involvement, watched worldly affair

Grief

There was a cry of losing someone owing to death,
The long-time sick mother of children six,
There was a chorus of sadness and, the scream deepest,
The kids felt dejected and were fear-ridden.

The girl was crying to call her mother back,
But nature was not empowered to accept that,
I prayed in vain to God for a miracle,
But alas! The slave nature is bound to follow the very fact.

The cry was becoming louder and louder,
It was acquiring tragic tune of the worst incident,
There was no one, and impossible to console each other,
Nothing can erase the memory, so persistent.

Younger children were terrified with tears,
Looking at the face of the elder sisters to find their mother,
They looked up to the sky in doubt and to the father,
To find the same assuring affection in the eyes of the elder.

Some said, 'Father is a stranger in the absence of the mother,
But he appeared tough and had a heart tender,
For small kids, he was a harsh figure.
Many felt sympathy and nothing more.'

Earth is the mother of all but delegated, it appears,
The responsibilities of being a mother,
Perhaps easily to all womankind of nature,
For being a store of love and the shelter.

Setting Sun Of The Year

Setting sun of the year,
With its scattering image in the river,
Going into the subconscious deeper,
Perhaps in the unconscious mind's quiver.

The next day rises on the surface of the mind,
Awareness of the memories unwinds,
To accept the future with eyes blind,
With a ray of hope and past behind.

Past depression and feelings of fury,
Buried deep in mind weary,
Under the deep waters, scary,
That past for which I feel sorry.

Pleasure mixed on the waves,
Rewinding life in the dark caves,
Fear not, though my mind braves,
The future is what the present craves.

Nature

Scattered pollen grains on the blossomed flower,
Spreads the seed of life, the tiny bee, bearer,
Hopping merely from flower to flower,
Not knowing, it is nature's life carrier.

The radiating sun and vaporizing ocean,
Taking the water to the heavenly station,
Pours rains to grow life, nature's mission,
Water seeps into the soil for vegetation.

Birds collect tiny grass and build an incredible nest,
What suits their needs, they do create the best.
Everyone has hidden treasure that they manifest,
Things take shape as per the artist's keen interest.

Which force is preparing for the life to come?
Who is working behind to give new life a home?
Food, safety, love and all that handsome,
Who is inspiring so to lead a life such awesome?

Dream

The vegetation standing steady in one place,
Dreamed of motion and wind, they embrace,
Longed to be open to the world with senses,
The creator understood it with good grace.

Created animals moving on the earth and water,
Gave them food and for defending unique features,
They, in turn, did wish to be better and better,
Dream for more and inspired the adventure.

Inside they dreamed of mind and intellect,
And humans did come into the race to be perfect,
Whatever they conceived created the subject,
Reaching into the inner space, the focus they direct.

Who created the first object and creatures?
Who pumped the spirit in the mere structures?
Who gave dreams to the animals for the features?
Who transforms, evolves, and fulfils the desires?

Turbulent

The turbulent ocean,
High waves,
Roaring sound,
Me standing,
Lonely on the beach.
Something similar wilder in mind,
The Sea is trying to reach the moon,
The way I did for you.
Contour on the beach
Is confining.
Self-imposed restrictions for me,
Waves break on the rocks.
Looking scared,
Like the outbursts in my mind.
I cannot meet you,
Neither can I see you
Again.
Thunder and lightning,
Something is striking
And I am crashing!

Liars

When all the liars came together,
Making appearance sincere,
With a look and feel of a factual white colour,
Wishing the fall of truth forever.

Some do get dark red emotions,
Friendly yellow and glorious green,
And the Hat of Hypocrisy in common,
Cheering loud, small victories they won.

Phrases that are common and traditional,
Borrowed from the trite words occasional,
Acting as if their view is final,
In the contents, nothing original.

Lies are but pieces of truth in parts,
Clad with colours and words of all sorts,
Truth gives vision even to the blind,
Lies make us blind through a gesture of any kind.

My Own Self

In my own body, I lost myself. Why?
Engaged in finding who I am.
With happy moments, I did fly,
When I witness grief still, I did try.

Filled with love and great passion,
Feelings and thoughts had the fusion,
I forgot myself while singing in unison,
Every form was my own version.

Sometimes satisfied with what I got,
Or disappointed but still dreamed a lot,
Excited about everything I bought,
But the answer for myself was what I sought.

Tried to find me in every mental occurrence,
Inseparable like flower and fragrance,
In my mind, feelings create resonance,
Can the self arise and show me once?

Freedom

The touch of the free air conveys freedom to my soul,
Free will reflects the freedom from things whole.
It is in search of ways of free-living as its purpose sole.
Free from desires, worries and fear in the performance of a role.

Rustling leaves make movements free and speak the freedom,
Though bound to the stem and within the limit, move random,
Free behaviour in my living, thought, and act deviates seldom,
But follows the liberty, hold it high and be restricted with wisdom.

Nature bestowed free will and freedom as a privilege,
To honour the freedom of others, we are under the pledge.
It is the virtue that has its place in life's central stage,
How we hold it and treat others, the universe acknowledges.

Liberal play of emotions did reflect in your eyes dark blue,
A tender love you gave me, and my freedom I gave you,
Use of might insult freedom, and the struggle and conflict continues,
Freedom of thought does uncover the truth and spreads it, in my view.

Wanderer

Images of the outside world, I see in the pond of mind.
The intense feeling of being, and I am sprayed with the wet wind.

On the surface of the pond, I try to search for my image sheer,
Ripples do distort it, or the violent waves make it disappear.

Experiences of the world whisper and make understanding clear,
Springs of consciousness originate within me, somewhere.

Eagerness to find the self, either deny the self or impose,
Either rebellious or instinctively loyal, to see the purpose.

There is no one else here; images do talk with me alone,
Existence relating to spring's origin and struggle of my own.

The springs, the pond of mind, and I am looking for me,
Existence, experience and discovery, I am wanderer free.

Spirit

When shall my true spirit speak?
That will be life's moment at its peak.
Show my destiny and answer my mind weak,
Does it have fixed rules or are there free ways to seek?

In the conversation, shall I ask the where about,
Of my being before birth and such doubt,
Am I a lone traveller, or do I have some defined route,
Am I whole like a seed or the part that sprouts?

My spirit will know and answer, I am sure,
Since I believe it witnesses me everywhere,
Even when I am sleeping, it is awake and aware,
It is present in the body and is in cells everywhere.

Forms of my inner existence who has chosen,
Who gives the stimulus and actions are driven,
Am I acting with free will or controlled by someone,
Is there a purpose, or is life but random events that happen?

Prayer

Oh, God! Help me cure
My mind, with a hardened layer,
Of insults, suffering, debility, and fear,
Submerged in lust and darkness,
Enslaved in the fight for existence mere!

Oh, God! Help me open
My mind missing light of the soul my own,
Eclipsed with desires and worldly goals,
Wandering in the darkness, lost illumination,
Deafened to the thoughts and acumen.

Oh, God! Help me sensitize
The elegiac tune of the life,
Does not bring tears to the eyes,
Help me from the mud to rise,
And see outward, awaken and arise!

Oh, God! Help me end
The past gloomy trend,
I see death as hope and life as punishment,
Oh, God! Bestow me the wings,
To fly and transcend.

Hermit

Monsoons poured down on him heavily,
And winters he endured,
In summer, he sweated,
But continued his penance.
All the desires arose and retired,
Hunger and thirst he bore,
Images he watched without involving,
Schemes of mind, thus, he made futile,
With an immense will, he thought he rose above nature's will.

He observed his own position.
Where self was leading the mind,
And walking over the memories,
The impressions of days and nights,
Of just watching them come and go,
Of unquenched thirst and hunger,
The volcanoes of passing desires,
Erupting and calming all by themselves,
Without affecting him a bit.
He lived alone and aloof, a true hermit!

Not knowing losing the self,
For the sake of love,
In an unaware or overwhelming moment.
Not knowing complying with nature,
Under the influence of instincts,
Does it also lead to realizing the truth?
He treated all nature's plays as
Inimical to his goal of freeing his soul,
He embarked on dominating nature.

By chance or as decreed by destiny,
Made his eyes meet with the nymph,
That image pierced through the defense,
He had created around his mind.
Her enticing beauty made magic,
He was but naught!
Alluring beauty spelt the incantation.
Till the depth of mind, he can see, but the image.
In the dark abyss of the mind, he saw
But her magnetic appearance.

He twisted his body in pain.
The eyes were stressed, dripped a few tears.
The third eye of the mind was lingering,
On the stubborn image that was still persisting.
The penance of the hermit was submerged,

In the illusory waters of the nature.

A sorrowful salty tear of the soul,

Weighed against nature's might whole.

He laid himself in the water,

Till the hermit's soul escaped nature!

Joyous Tree

The rainwater is dripping,
Through the leaves of a tree.
Me still standing below,
Shivering with each drop falling,
Stuck in the place,
Being already wet.
Water filtering through the leaves,
And mixing love from the tree.
Making me startle and wonder,
Whether the tree has age-old affection.
Wet leaves are playing mischief,
And drawing my attention.
The scattering rays on the leaves,
Expressing their joyfulness,
And the damp trunk of the tree,
Despite having some cuts,
And wet wounds in some places,
Was too smiling.

Picture

A river flows with ripples, wreathing a hill,
Wet rocks on the way bathed with a fresh feel,
Green trees tall on the way, standing still,
The wind blows, hinting to fly with free will.

What is the secret of the beauty spread so serene?
The climax is absent, and the song is there so divine,
Artist is missing, and the elegant work is so fine,
Wonder who and for whom has created the picturesque scene.

Trees with yellow leaves are so charming,
I draw the face of my yellow-dressed darling,
The trunk is the body and leaves the attire eye-catching,
Resting on the cushion of air with legs stretching.

Does the Creator become obscure?
To let the mind discover the enjoyer,
And allow Him to empower,
To draw in mind a complete picture.

Tree

My roots cling to the soil,
I suck my spirit from the water.
I am standing on my trunk,
And spread in the ether.
My leaves chatter with the air,
Flowers allure bees,
Honey is my love,
Flower's scent I give to the world.
And my fruit's juice is my goodness,
Its sweetness I give to the world.
I have never asked who I am.
Or where am I to go?
For I am standing in my place,
I see my seeds sown in the ground,
I give what I take,
Even while am being burnt.

Dew

Scattering rays from the dew,
On the petal, wet and blue,
What a tiny treasure new!
And the new morning view.

Has night gifted the tiny crystal?
Working with a divine miracle,
To the morning making so special,
The charming spark is so gentle.

Can it be woven into a garland?
With the thread of sunrays and,
Give the creator offering grand,
The magic woven with my hand.

Can I reduce myself to a form so tiny?
Where my spirit is that shiny,
The leaf holding me and my destiny,
And my body, the dew watery.

Oh, Love!

Oh, Love! What all colours do you wear?
What is the colour when the lovers swear?
Sometimes showing no colours or reflecting multi-colour?
Often ends merrily and sometimes brings a tear.

You are bashful red on the cheeks of the sweetheart,
Grey, black or brown hair and the face looks so bright,
Dark complexion or fair one and the glow with divine art,
Colourless in the lucid eyes but captivating of the sort!

Sometimes you lead the lovers to a happy destination,
Or make them face bitter truth and frustration.
Still, they look at each other and fulfil minds with affection.
Many may call it madness, but they have a brave reaction.

O love, you are the creation of the world divine,
You are the force that makes everyone align,
You reflect in every attraction benign,
You are the highest virtue in every heart that shines.

The Whole And Parts

The whole is divided into dual,
Light and darkness are both real,
Man is a machine, and food is fuel,
Truth is but unknown actual.

The whole is compelled for survival.
Parts struggle for the other part.
Life is all that perfection trial.
Moments of parting and unison, loyal.

What is life meant for the whole?
What truth plays the role?
Or everything real is the sole,
A puzzle dwelling in a black hole.

So many paths and ways tried,
In unison, although satisfied,
With no answers, the mind is void,
With no questions, life is void.

Death, Who Are You?

It was a death that was the appealing void,
Time was running, but awareness was devoid,
Cells detaching from my body on air to ride,
Beyond light and darkness, the whole world aside.

The heart can't beat for romance,
Legs, checkmate on dead stance,
Hands, no work to do, no chance,
Brain, no thoughts, not even in a trance.

Mind left desires aside,
No instincts upon to ride,
No sweet, or bitter taste, palate died,
No mental occurrence abides.

The brain doesn't classify as wrong or right,
Doesn't qualify significant or slight,
Doesn't measure zero or infinite,
No joining of loose dots tight.

The self, do not imagine flocks uniting in one,
Doesn't reflect on where reason is none,
Doesn't accept where all are falsity clones,
Doesn't compete with others since you are alone.

Paused me in the rush of the world,
The flow of the blood was ice cold,
Breathing in lungs with the aching fold,
The Future was nothing and the past in junk hold.

One day, you die; you are to die.
And so, what is death? Question not why,
Can you reincarnate within life to freshly fly?
To inquire about death, what does life imply?

Identity

Is my life a dream to my real me?
Am I outside the world that I can see?
At a centre of a circle, I exist, free,
Beyond all dimensions, I am so tiny.

I carry my body, a machine of a kind,
See the world, involve, and bind.
Invisible in the cells myself do I find.
I watch myself in the mirror of my mind.

Delusion of being aware from within,
That cries and laughs and listens keenly,
Is it me, true or false, a difference thin?
Sometimes that isolates, control and reign.

I don't really exist. Sometimes I feel,
Mind is tied to nature's wheel,
Where am I to go? It does not reveal,
Identity of mine, why does it conceal?

Joy

Spread the wings and fly in the inner space of the mind,
Joy emerging from within and patterns one of a kind.

The rays of the sun falling on a tree and the shadows of leaves,
Blocked by the worries and fear, feel the calm that bliss gives.

Captivated self and confined mind in settling all the dues,
Lost in the routine, feeble you, limiting the wider views.

Early morning, and greens on which fresh dew is sprayed,
New horizon dark and light, and colours of different shed.

The night sky, moonshine and twinkling stars at infinite distance,
Whether it is joy or sorrow, it is always a new occurrence.

Ease the sight, fill the mind with all the inner radiance,
Passage of time will make it normal, any bitter incidence.

Learned

Learned were defining the wisdom,
As the ability to succeed and decide,
Where data and facts agree,
Judge by what guts feel about,
Within the constraints that fit,
Get the focus right,
No place for conflict,
Eliminate that from the root.
You can't please everyone.
Goals, methods and means,
Sense of time and place wins,
And so on…
Upon finishing, the man asked.
His wife, who was listening,
'What is wisdom?'
Said his wife,
'I collect the material for cooking,
Cut the vegetables, put the oil and fry,
Knead the dough and shape it,
And then heat,
Don't complain if my finger is cut,
Neither if my hand is burnt,

With a proportion of items right,
Cook the food that arises appetite.
Help everyone get ready in time,
Love everyone, manage egos,
But don't know what wisdom is.'

Debris

Debris in my mind,
Accumulated with age.
To throw away and keep clean,
Need space for the garbage.

Memories worth throwing away,
Forgotten but still surface as tendencies,
Images daunting and dancing,
Sources challenging to trace.

I frequent the dumping ground,
To discard the trash and burn it,
In my mind, though can't help,
The foul smell persist.

The memories are blessed with oblivion,
But once stored can't eradicate,
I condition my mind and relax,
Lighten the candle and meditate.

Wisdom

I am unable to define wisdom,
Whether it is present in the heart that loves,
Or the brain that thinks,
Or the mind that senses and feels,
Or the self that controls.
Thinking without a conclusion is not wisdom.
A love that blinds does not see the truth.
And ignorant love can even be fatal.
The mind goes by what pleases it,
And self is often clouded by ego.
Then what perceives the truth?
To understand the mind and converge thoughts,
To understand heart and control,
Wisdom is a pillar.
Is it merely a perception that provides views?
Is it a strength to act?
Merely work, work and work?
Or considers rewards too?
Are there infinite variables in the equation?
And the truth is the ultimate conclusion.
Process of deriving truth,
A faculty needs a separate provision.

Fullmoon

The full moon reflected in the mirror of the mind,
Milky waves of moonlight, of tranquil kind
Invisible inner sphere filled, I did find,
With pleasant warmth that of the scented wind.

The charming mind is so deep and mysterious,
Whether awake or dreamy, the state is not obvious,
Every moment contains feelings harmonious,
Oneness with everything appearing spontaneous.

Both the hands tied in the tasks worldly,
Now forgotten and given up living outwardly,
The journey has started towards riches inwardly,
No desires and deserted the mind suddenly.

No subjects exist, and the withdrawn senses,
Enlightened eyes inward filled with images,
It was mere existence and pure consciousness,
For the meaningful self, everything else was meaningless.

Horizon

The boundary of my existence,
Where my small world ends,
As I rise higher,
It expands but still exists.
The sun rises on my horizon,
Birds do fly in flocks,
Twinkling stars spread,
The moon ascends,
In the sky.
Horizon,
Where my limits meet,
My thoughts may rise high,
Heart enlarge,
My Soul shed its flashes,
That is my little space,
Surrounded by the infinite around,
And infinite stars cast their tiny spots,
In my mysterious sky.

Hope

Mother of all instincts plays,
Life arises hope before birth,
The child makes efforts to stand,
Without knowing why,
Hidden hope plays its role,
Continues effort till it walks.

When the bleak phase of life starts,
It feels like no hope is there.
Know it does not disappear,
It influences different avenues,
Reflects secrets of the soul,
Inspired by the spirit of living.

At a time, how many feelings do we feel?
Some comfortable and some frightening,
Some felt clear, and some obscure mixtures,
Sometimes so intense forcing to stop and end.
Hope diverts you and balances,
When stable, it asks to take one step ahead.

When desperation tries to occupy the mind,
The force of life carries hope,
A feeling of hope is a mystery
When everything is lost, hope remains,
And when hope is lost, the soul springs it again,
It remains there till the soul departs.

Magnificent Lady!

Oh, Magnificent lady, your gaze,
Have a coolness and as well as a fire,
Enslave but earn respect,
That crushes and also gratifies,
Your eyes enchant and fascinate,
Also, sober up, who dares drink from it,
Your swagger and proud movement,
Also, accompany polite and deep touch,
Eyes turning red with a tear, you move,
And disregard two-faced.
Quick wit feels sharper than a sword,
And the sense of humour burst the laughter.
Yes, you are born to be superior,
You know not misery and compose the temper,
You are a moving pride, a wonder,
Oh, marvellous paradox, my mind oscillates,
You touch my soul deeper.

Structure

Objects came into existence and set into motion,
Relative to each other, they set the position,
Spinning around themselves and another one,
The fire perpetual further created composition.

The structures got complex and came with matter,
The force of attraction and repellent together,
Ether is in and around the whole whatsoever,
Fire transforms light, solid, liquid and air.

From where did the first fire come into existence?
From where did the first force come into existence?
Who dreamt of the structures taking such shapes?
And after fashioning all this, how He escapes?

Is there someone who first dreams?
The world it visualizes it seems,
Then the fire plots the themes,
And the Five elements implement schemes.

Darkness

I beheld the darkness
With my eyes open,
Where there is no star or a planet,
In the nearby skies,
Not used to seeing such,
Stagnant darkness.
Closed the eyes, but no difference,
Shouted in the loudest voice possible,
But nothing was heard, and no echo,
Surprised to realize even,
I am unable to touch me.
I am reduced to just,
That which is weightless,
And so infinitesimal,
Or like a wave moving bodiless,
Slowly drifting to nothingness,
That is a precursor to eternity.
Not sure how far the darkness was spread,
But I became one with it.
Not sure if I enclosed the darkness or
Darkness enclosed me,
No difference whatever be,
Is it that I am now a travelling spirit in eternity?

Drop Of Water

A drop of water fell on a rock by chance,
And set to vanish in vapour.
Again, to rise to the sky and,
Pour as rain with vigour.
When it fell into the ocean,
Swallowed forces of waves,
With winds, it flew across continents,
Became a life-giving breath of creatures.
Again, it went to the sky and poured,
Fell on the ground and absorbed.
Force of life was awaiting it,
A root of a tree swallowed it.
Oh, tiny life bearer,
You are a flood of emotions in the tear,
You are the sweat of the labour.
Oh, drop of water, sweet,
I hold you and promise,
I shall not waste and treat you wise.

Divine Design

On top of the hill below the sky,
Watching the birds together fly,
I was standing calm, know not why,
Stretching hands wider as if to fly.

Below in the valley, I can observe,
A majestic river forming a curve,
Design divine created with verve,
Filling the calmness in my nerve.

Green was descending from the hill,
From the ages standing still,
A spring pouring down so tranquil,
Nothing can disturb my mind nil.

Absorbed and mixed with the scene,
Stopped the senses with feelings so serene,
I was drinking the magic of marvellous wine,
Oneness but no other word to say what I seen.

Ant Heap

I can't dream of a home as marvellous as the ant heap,
So many holes and outlets, as mysterious and so deep,
Small and big many chambers where little food they keep,
After working the whole day, where do they really sleep?

No route is a dead end, and no jam takes place,
Who has built the paths where no one derails?
A wonderful place where only harmony dwells,
As if anyone goes down, the whole thing fails.

Layers one above the other, with their splendid peak,
The tiny fort looks so delicate but not so weak,
So many places hidden and so easy to trick,
Can I become an ant and play inside hide and seek.

I am an alone dweller, and my mind is a hill,
Climbing up and down, I do the drill,
Travel through the tunnels and enjoy the feel,
Play with me, hide and seek, the never-ending thrill!

I Have Faith In

Whether the universe is finite or infinite,
I have faith in
My small world around me,
That is the universe for me, though slight.

Whether time is finite or infinite,
I have faith in
The fewer years of my lifetime,
That is the span for me complete.

Whether there is an afterlife or not,
I have faith in
My life came to me by chance,
That is the stage for me to act a lot.

Whether God exists or not,
I have faith in
The love that connects all and one,
Never seen it empty, the nectar pot.

Whether there is a purpose for life or not,
I have faith in
The constant struggle to face the life,
And feel proud of the rewards I got.

Whether I have an answer to who am I?
I have faith in
Conscience, Confidence, and being aware,
With virtues and courage, routes I can try.